BECOMING
A WOMAN OF
GRACE

CYNTHIA HEALD

NELSON IMPACT
A Division of Thomas Nelson Publishers
Since 1798

www.thomasnelson.com

Published in Nashville, Tennessee, by Thomas Nelson, Inc.

Published in association with the literary agency of Alive Communications, 1465 Kelly Johnson Blvd., Suite 320, Colorado Springs, CO 80920.

Scripture quotations noted *The Message* are from *The Message: The New Testament in Contemporary English.* Copyright © 1993 by Eugene H. Peterson.

Scripture quotations noted NASB are taken from the NEW AMERICAN STANDARD BIBLE®. Copyright © The Lockman Foundation 1960, 1962, 1963, 1968, 1971, 1972, 1973, 1975, 1977. Used by permission.

Scripture quotations noted NIV are from the HOLY BIBLE: NEW INTER-NATIONAL VERSION®. Copyright © 1973, 1978, 1984 by International Bible Society. Used by permission of Zondervan Publishing House. All rights reserved.

Scripture quotations noted NLT are taken from the *Holy Bible,* New Living Translation, copyright © 1996. Used by permission of Tyndale House Publishers, Inc., Wheaton, Illinois 60189. All rights reserved.

Scripture quotations noted PHILLIPS are from J. B. Phillips: THE NEW TES-TAMENT IN MODERN ENGLISH. Revised Edition. Copyright © J. B. Phillips 1958, 1960, 1972. Used by permission of Macmillan Publishing Co., Inc.

The material credited to Jerry Bridges in Chapters 4, 7, and 8 is reprinted from *Transforming Grace,* copyright © 1991 by Jerry Bridges. Used by permission of NavPress, Colorado Springs, CO. All rights reserved. For copies call (800) 366-7788. The material credited to Jerry Bridges in Chapter 11 is reprinted from *The Practice of Godliness,* copyright © 1983 by Jerry Bridges. Used by permission of NavPress, Colorado Springs, CO. All rights reserved. For copies call 800-366-7788.

ISBN 0-7852-7240-2

Printed in the United States of America.
26 27 RRD 08 07

CONTENTS

How to Use This Guide

This Bible study has been created to help you search the Scriptures and draw closer to God as you seek to understand, experience, and reflect His grace. All you need is a Bible, a writing tool, and an expectant heart. You may find it helpful, however, to have access to a supplemental resource such as a general commentary, Bible handbook, or a study Bible with reference notations.

Becoming a Woman of Grace is appropriate for individual as well as group use, and for women of any age and season of life. Before you begin each chapter, pray for attentiveness to how God is speaking to you through His Word and for sensitivity to His prompting. At the conclusion of each chapter, you will have opportunity to write out a prayer as a way of verbalizing your response to the Lord and drawing closer to Him. Choosing to memorize the suggested Scripture passages will help you abide in Christ day by day as His truth dwells deep within your mind and heart.

The Bible has much to say about the importance of learning from and encouraging one another in the community of believers. If you are using this study with a small group, the questions and prayers will give you excellent opportunities for talking and praying together about appropriating God's grace.

The quotations from Christian writers have been selected to help you understand the biblical content of each chapter and to enhance your personal response to God's Word. Consider using the Notes section in the back of this book as a resource list for further devotional reading and study.

As you come to the Father and Child dialogues that open and close this study of grace, read them prayerfully as a means of drawing closer to the heart of God.

$\mathcal{P}$REFACE

Amazing grace—how sweet the sound! *Grace* is a lovely word and a prized attribute, manifesting itself in steadfast kindness and benevolence. To be known as a gracious person is a high compliment.

It was last year that I felt led to write a Bible study on grace. I actually had another topic in mind, but the Lord seemed to say quite clearly, "Cynthia, it is time that you learned about grace." So began my immersion into the vast ocean of God's unmerited favor. It often seemed that I was treading these gracious waters looking for the shore—for grace itself is infinitely deep.

This study has probably been the hardest to write of any I have embarked upon. I have read more commentators, deleted more sentences, and rearranged more chapters than in the development of any other guide. I have to smile while recalling how the Lord whispered in my heart along the way that I would have a personal testimony to His grace when I finished! Because of unexpected circumstances in my life coinciding with the time set aside for this writing, I have experienced the freshness and abundance of God's grace in completing this undertaking. The conversations between the Father and the Child arose as He led me to a deeper understanding of His loving faithfulness.

I pray that you will discover new facets of grace and experience new areas of freedom in your life. To glimpse the fullness of His grace is a life-changing revelation. May His grace so infuse your heart and direct your life that others will be blessed as you become a woman of grace.

Grace to you!

Love in Christ,

Cynthia Heald

The Father and the Child

The Father spoke:

Dear child, it is time for you to understand My grace.

Yes, Father; I know little of Your grace.

If you do not begin to comprehend the depth and
breadth of My grace, you will not live in the freedom
and holiness that I have purposed for you.

I want to live fully as You have intended.

My grace to you came at a great cost, and I desire that
you become a woman of grace.

How will I learn of Your grace?

By listening carefully to My Word, drawing close to
Me in prayer, and allowing My Spirit to teach you.
Come, child, let us begin. I long to show you My
graciousness.

CHAPTER 1
GOD IS GRACIOUS

Therefore the LORD *longs to be gracious*
to you,
And therefore He waits on high to have
compassion on you.
For the LORD *is a God of justice;*
How blessed are all those who long
for Him.

Isaiah 30:18 NASB

Before sin entered the world, Adam and Eve experienced God's goodness not as a response to their demerit (since they didn't have any) but still without deserving God's goodness. You can't deserve to be created. You can't deserve, as a non-being, to be put into a lavish garden where all your needs are met by a loving Father. So even before they sinned, Adam and Eve lived on grace. And God's will for them was that they live by faith in future grace—God's daily, fatherly care and provision.[1]

John Piper

$\mathcal{F}$rom its opening pages Scripture shows us that God has always longed to be gracious. His creation of a marvelous world out of nothing is amazing evidence of His grace, and He placed His children in it to be recipients of His grace. In the garden, Adam and Eve were immersed in God's goodness. They did nothing to earn their place there, and they did nothing to receive His love. God simply chose to be kind, merciful, and compassionate to them. Charles Ryrie observes, "God's love for man is the first motive for His acting in grace on behalf of man."[2] From creation onward we find that God has showered upon us His undeserved favor. Truly He is the God of all grace.

God's Smile

1. Just as God in His sovereignty chose to create Adam and Eve in order to love them, He also created relationship with His chosen people in order to love them. Read Deuteronomy 7:6–11 and record the evidences of Israel's undeserved favor.

2. Derek Kidner portrays Old Testament grace as the "smile of God."[3] Read the verses below and describe God's "smile" on Noah, Abram, Jacob, and Joseph.

Genesis 6:5–8

Genesis 12:1–3

Genesis 33:1–11 (Jacob was meeting Esau for the first time after years of estrangement following Jacob's theft of Esau's birthright.)

Genesis 39:19–23 (Joseph, sold into slavery in Egypt by his brothers, had become a servant to Potiphar, whose wife falsely accused him of attempting to seduce her.)

The word *favor* is the nearest Biblical synonym for the word *grace*. In this connection it may be observed that the one thought which is almost exclusively expressed in the New Testament by the word *grace*, is, in the Old Testament, almost exclusively expressed by the word *favor*. *Grace is favor, and favor is grace. Thus, in considering the Bible teaching on this great theme, equal attention should be given to all passages wherein either the word grace is used or favor is found.* Grace means pure unrecompensed kindness and favor.[4]

Lewis Sperry Chafer

God's Favor

3. Moses was privileged to hear the Lord speak to him "face to face." Record God's communication of His grace to Moses in Exodus 33:11–23.

So right at the center of God's self revelation is the declaration that he is free in the way he dispenses his grace. And this freedom belongs to the very essence of what it means to be God. God is gracious to whom he will be gracious. He is not limited by anyone's wickedness. He is never trapped by his own wrath. His grace may break out anywhere he pleases.[5]

John Piper

4. The psalmist David has given us some of the greatest testimonials to God's grace in all of Scripture. Read Psalm 103 and summarize David's characterizations of God's graciousness to himself and others.

Psalm 103:1–14

5. David prompts us in Psalm 103 to remember God's benefits. Write down some of God's "benefits," or ways in which He has shown His graciousness to you.

6. Isaiah relates God's response to rebellious Judah in Isaiah 30:8–19. Describe Judah's rebellion and God's response.

Judah's rebellion:

God's response:

> He will wait to be gracious; he will wait till you return to him and seek his face, and then he will be ready to meet you with mercy. He will wait, that he may do it in the best and fittest time, when it will be most for his glory, when it will come to you with the most pleasing surprise. He will continually follow you with his favours, and not let slip any opportunity to be gracious to you.[6]
>
> *Matthew Henry*

Author's Reflection

I'll never forget an unpleasant experience I had in junior high school. I was invited over to a friend's house for lunch after church, and as we were eating, my friend and her dad got into an argument. I was appalled when he jumped up from the table in a fit of anger, stormed over to where she was sitting, and slapped her. Afterward, I tried to comfort her while she cried. I also decided that I never wanted to return for another visit to her home.

Sadly, many fathers are harsh with their children. Consequently, it is easy to view God as a stern figure who is easily provoked to rage and quick to punish. Many people struggle to see Him as anything more than a judge waiting to pass sentence on their sins and lack of perfection. This mistaken understanding of God's character hinders our trust and surrender to our Lord. God is righteous and He does exercise justice, but His actions are characterized by grace, mercy, and compassion. He chooses to be gracious, He longs to be gracious—even to disobedient children. He patiently waits to manifest His grace.

"Never be sympathetic with the soul whose case makes you come to the conclusion that God is hard," advises Oswald Chambers. "God is more tender than we can conceive. . . ."[7] And this is our God. He would never act as my friend's father did, striking out in rage. Even when He chastens us in the midst of our sin and unfaithfulness, He does so with loving patience and always for our good. We, who repeatedly ignore the instruction of the Lord and by our actions say, "Stop confronting us with the Holy One of Israel" (Isa. 30:11 NIV), are undeserving. Yet God earnestly *waits* to be gracious and to show us mercy and loving-kindness. How blessed are all those who long for Him, for they will experience His grace.

All that God wanted man to do was to believe in Him. What a man believes, moves and rules his whole being, enters into him, and becomes part of his very life. Salvation could only be by faith: God restoring the life man had lost; man in faith yielding himself to God's work and will. The first great work of God with man was to get him to believe. This work cost God more care and time and patience than we can easily conceive. All the dealings with individual men, and with the people of Israel, had just this one object, to teach men to trust Him. Where He found faith He could do anything. Nothing dishonoured and grieved Him so much as unbelief. Unbelief was the root of disobedience and every sin; it made it impossible for God to do His work. The one thing God sought to waken in men by promise and threatening, by mercy and judgment, was faith.

Of the many devices of which God's patient and condescending grace made use to stir up and strengthen faith, one of the chief was—the Covenant.[8]

Andrew Murray

Amazing Grace

7. "The supreme divine objective is, then, that infinite love may manifest itself in superabounding grace," writes Lewis Sperry Chafer.[9] Take time to write a prayer asking God to lead you into a deeper understanding of His boundless grace in your life.

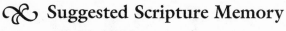 **Suggested Scripture Memory**
Isaiah 30:18

CHAPTER 2

Covenants of a Gracious God

> *"But this is the new covenant I will make with the people of Israel on that day," says the* Lord. *"I will put my laws in their minds, and I will write them on their hearts. I will be their God, and they will be my people."*
>
> Jeremiah 31:33 NLT

And so the Covenant was, above all, to give man *a hold upon God, as* the Covenant-keeping God, to link him to God Himself in expectation and hope, to bring him to make God Himself alone the portion and the strength of his soul.[1]

Andrew Murray

To know that God makes binding agreements, or "covenants," with His people is necessary for understanding His grace. "A biblical covenant," writes Lawrence Richards, "is a clear statement of God's purposes and intentions expressed in terms that bind God by solemn oath to perform what he has promised."[2] Whenever God promises to His people that He will do something, He takes the initiative in making the promise as well as the responsibility for ensuring that it will be carried out. If He did not take the initiative, we would not know Him. We can look at God's covenants as proclamations of His desire to enter into relationship with us. They are extraordinary indications that God has bound Himself to us forever. They are for our benefit, not His—they give us "a hold upon Him" so that we might cling to Him in confidence that He extends His favor to us of His own free choice.

God's Faithfulness

1. After the Flood, God made a covenant with Noah and his sons. Read Genesis 9:8–17 and write down God's promise, to whom it was made, and the sign accompanying the covenant.

2. God appeared to Abram as "God Almighty," or "the Abundant One," and declared His covenant with him. From the following Scripture, write down God's promises to Abram and the sign of this covenant.

Genesis 17:1–11 (See also Ps. 105:8–15.)

3. David desired to build a house for God, but instead God made an everlasting covenant with him. Read 2 Samuel 7:8–17 and write down God's promise to David. (For additional insight, read Ps. 89:20–37.)

Combining these ideas of intensity and relationship, it is plain to see that when God shows His *chesed* [one of the principal Old Testament words for grace] in a covenant relationship, His grace is firm, persistent and steadfast . . . thus the thought of faithfulness, not the ideas of kindness and mercy, predominates in the grace relationship.[3]

Charles Ryrie

God's Instruction

4. After God delivered Israel from their bondage in Egypt, for their protection and well-being He gave the nation a set of laws to live by. (The heart of this law, or Mosaic covenant, is found in Ex. 20:1–17.) Read Exodus 19:1–6 and summarize the purpose and terms of this covenant that God made with His people through Moses.

The basic biblical covenants are the Abrahamic, the Mosaic, the Davidic, and the new. All but the Mosaic covenant look forward to history's end for their ultimate fulfillment. The Mosaic covenant was a temporary covenant, the constitution of the nation Israel. It was based on human effort, not on promise, for its performance. It was intended to define for Israel the lifestyle that would enable God to bless them until the new covenant was made.[4]

Lawrence O. Richards

5. God was continually faithful to guide His people and to provide for them. What does Jeremiah 11:7–8 indicate about whether Israel kept her side of the agreement?

6. Even though Israel broke covenant, God did not forsake His people. How did His response, as communicated in Jeremiah 31:33–34, reveal His faithfulness as a covenant-keeping God?

7. God's desire is always to guide His children in the best way. How would you describe the differences between the new covenant God announced to Jeremiah and the old covenant He gave through Moses?

And this now is the reason why there was a first and a second covenant, that in the first, man's desires and efforts might be fully awakened, and time given for him to make full proof of what his human nature, with the aid of outward instruction and miracles and means of grace, could accomplish. When his utter impotence, his hopeless captivity under the power of sin had been discovered, there came the New Covenant, in which God was to reveal how man's true liberty from sin and self and the creature, his true nobility and God-likeness, was to be found in the most entire and absolute dependence, in God's being and doing all within him.[5]

Andrew Murray

COVENANTS OF A GRACIOUS GOD

8. Taking into account God's gracious character, why do you think He chose to proclaim a new covenant?

Author's Reflection

As a little girl, I remember saying, "I cross my heart and hope to die!" I used this phrase to emphasize and legitimize the truth and sincerity of a statement I had just made. Sometimes, if I wanted to tease someone or test her gullibility by telling her something that wasn't true, I would cross my fingers behind my back as a way of absolving myself from telling a lie.

When God speaks, and particularly when He makes a promise, He does not need to add an oath to verify His word. And we need never worry that He crosses His fingers behind His back. Numbers 23:19 tells us, "God is not a man, that he should lie. He is not a human, that he should change his mind. Has he ever spoken and failed to act? Has he ever promised and not carried it through?" (NLT).

God's covenants represent His intense longing to be our God and to draw us into intimate relationship with Him. He has stated clearly and boldly His desire for how His children should live. The Mosaic covenant spelled out the way the Israelites were to order their lives. The problem was not in God's provision, but in Israel's response. Israel continually abandoned God, worshiping idols and refusing to repent. They "broke" covenant.

God had Jeremiah announce a new covenant—one in which the law would be in the heart of man. To inaugurate this new covenant, God would send His own Son. The apostle John wrote, "So the word of God became a human being and lived among us. We saw his glory (the glory like that of a father's only son), full of grace and truth" (John 1:14 PHILLIPS).

God is a covenant-keeping God. As evidence, we have rainbows, the nation of Israel and Abraham's spiritual descendants, an established throne of David through Christ, and a new covenant sealed by the blood of Christ. These are all confirmations of God's eternal faithfulness and extravagant grace—no fingers behind my back, cross my heart and hope to die.

[The] law witnessed to our great salvation in Christ through types. The entire sacrificial system of the Mosaic law pointed forward to the Lamb of God who taketh away the sin of the world. Thus the law spoke clearly and unmistakably of a divine righteousness bestowed by the grace of God on those who simply believe, while at the same time the law could not make the slightest contribution to that righteousness. The correct formula, therefore, is divine

righteousness apart from law but witnessed by the law. The law had only the "shadow of good things to come," but "not the very image" of those things (Heb. 10:1). Let us recognize the value of the shadow, but let us beware even of seeming to put one iota of the shadow in the place of the substance.[6]

Alva J. McClain

Amazing Grace

9. Andrew Murray wrote, "God was ever to take the initiative, and be to man the source of life."[7] Reflect on how God has taken the initiative in your life, and write out a prayer of gratitude.

 **Suggested Scripture Memory**

Jeremiah 31:33

CHAPTER 3

The Law and the New Covenant

❧

But when the right time came, God sent his Son, born of a woman, subject to the law. God sent him to buy freedom for us who were slaves to the law, so that he could adopt us as his very own children.

Galatians 4:4–5 NLT

Had Christ come directly after the fall, the enormity and deadly fruits of sin would not have been realized fully by man, so as to feel his desperate state and need of a Savior. Sin was fully developed. Man's inability to save himself by obedience to the law, whether that of Moses, or that of conscience, was completely manifested; all the prophecies of various ages found their common center in *this* particular time and Providence, by various arrangements in the social and political, as well as the moral world, had fully prepared the way for the coming Redeemer.[1]

*G*od's law was originally written on stone—a set of instructions for righteous conduct established for Israel's good. Scripture tells us that the law was given as a tutor, to teach us godly living (Gal. 3:24). Blessings from the hand of God would result as His people obeyed and walked in His commandments. Although Israel knew what was right, over and over again they rebelled and disobeyed. "If we ask what was missing from the hearts of so many who heard the law and failed to walk in it," observes John Piper, "one clear biblical answer is that *faith* was missing. . . . Again and again this is the missing ingredient in the Old Testament that short-circuits obedience to God's commandments."[2]

The law was a witness to righteousness, but it had no power to make the people righteous because it did not produce faith. So God promised a new covenant, in which He would write His law in the people's hearts and then give them the power to keep it. In the fullness of time, the Mediator of the promised new covenant appeared. Jesus became the perfect sacrifice to fulfill the demands of the old covenant. He purchased our freedom so that we might be adopted as God's beloved children.

The Purpose of the Law

1. Scripture states that the law was intended to provide a standard of righteousness for the people. Read the following Scriptures and summarize what they say about the purpose of the law and the actual results it produced.

Romans 7:7–13

Galatians 3:19–29

The Old was, and was meant to be, a "ministration of death"; until it has completely done its work in us there is no complete discharge from its power. The man who sees that self is incurably evil and must die; who gives self utterly to death as he sinks before God in utter impotence and the surrender to His workings; who consents to death with

Christ on the cross as his desert, and in faith accepts it as his only deliverance; he alone is prepared to be led by the Holy Spirit into the full enjoyment of the New Covenant life. He will learn to understand how completely death makes an end to all self-effort, and how, as he lives in Christ to God, everything henceforth is to be the work of God Himself.[3]

Andrew Murray

2. The law foreshadowed the high priestly role of Christ. Read Hebrews 10:1–18. What does this passage teach about how Christ ushered in the new covenant?

The Fulfillment of the Law

3. In the Sermon on the Mount, Jesus spoke very directly concerning the law. Read Matthew 5:17–20 and summarize His teaching.

4. Paul wrote concerning the sufficiency of Christ's sacrifice in Romans 5:12–21. What are his key insights in this passage regarding sin and grace?

The word *fulfill* means "to fill out, expand, or complete." It does not mean to bring to an end. Jesus fulfills the law in several ways: (1) He obeyed it perfectly and taught its correct meaning; (2) He will one day fulfill all of the Old Testament types and prophesies; and (3) He provides a way of salvation that meets all the requirements of the law.[4]

5. In Christ, God graciously offers His children a new way of being in relationship with Him. How would you summarize the purpose of the law and Christ's fulfillment of it in this new relationship?

The Power of the New Covenant

6. The law could not help us live righteously. According to the following passages, how does the new covenant empower us to live as God wants us to?

Ezekiel 36:22–28

John 7:37–39

Titus 3:3–7

The basic difference between the old covenant offered by God through the law and the new covenant offered by God through Christ is not that one had commandments and the other doesn't. The basic difference is that in the old covenant the gracious enabling power to obey was not poured out as fully as it is since Jesus. . . . What's new about the new covenant is not that there is no law, but rather God's promise, "I will put My law within them, and on their heart I will write it" (Jer. 31:33). "I will put my spirit within you and cause you to walk in My statutes" (Ezek. 36:27).[5]

John Piper

Author's Reflection

Growing up, I was given money when I made straight A's in school. The message I got from this reward was that I needed to be perfect. If I earned a B, I felt that I had failed. My parents loved me and wanted me to do my best, but it was a weight to feel that I always had to achieve.

It was a great moment in my life when I realized that I no longer had to be perfect to be loved. I think this is the way anyone who begins to study the law and the new covenant must feel. Under the law, we are graded by how perfectly we obey it. Most of us know all too well, though, that we can never measure up. As Paul exclaimed, even when we know what is right to do, it's so very hard to do it. This is why the Israelites were continually required to offer sacrifices for failure.

But God gave the law so His children would understand what righteous living looked like, not to keep them subjected to Him in fear of failure. His great desire was for the people to love and serve Him with all their hearts. When the law had fulfilled its purpose in revealing our inadequacy to live righteously in our own strength, God Himself graciously made provision for the law to be fulfilled. He sent His Son to initiate a new covenant, opening a new way for His people to live wholeheartedly for Him.

This new covenant takes the responsibility of earning God's favor off our shoulders. We no longer have to strive for perfection on our own merits. Sacrifice is no longer demanded for failure; now, all that is needed is faith. We can be perfect in the sight of God because of Christ's sacrifice, once for all.

Under the old covenant, I was under pressure to perform. Under the new covenant, Jesus has taken my place. I can now rest in the assurance of God's love, and in His power to live a new life in me. The good news of the new covenant is that I am no longer in school, worrying about grades. I have graduated to grace.

The old proprietorship, the old life, must disappear entirely before the new heir, the new life, can enter upon the inheritance. Nothing but death can work the transference of the property. It is even so with Christ, with the Old and the New Covenant life, with our own deliverance from the Old and our entrance on the New. Now, having been made dead to the law by the body of Christ, we have been discharged from the law, having died to that wherein we were holden—here is the completeness of the deliverance from Christ's side; "so that we serve"—here is the completeness of the change in our experience—"in newness of the spirit, and not in oldness of the letter."[6]

Andrew Murray

Amazing Grace

7. Lewis Sperry Chafer observes, "Grace finds its greatest triumph and glory in the sphere of human helplessness."[7] Reflect on this statement in light of your helplessness to live righteously in your own strength. Then write out a prayer expressing your thoughts to the Lord regarding His covenant of grace.

℘ Suggested Scripture Memory

Galatians 4:4–5

CHAPTER 4

God's Gracious Salvation

*For by grace you have been saved through
faith; and that not of yourselves, it is the gift
of God; not as a result of works, that no one
should boast.*

Ephesians 2:8–9 NASB

It was because of His grace that God the Father sent His
only son to die in our place. To say it another way, Christ's
death was the result of God's grace; grace is not the result
of Christ's death. . . . Because Christ completely satisfied the justice of God, we can now experience the grace
of God.[1]

Jerry Bridges

*T*he law could not provide salvation or justification (that is, to be declared righteous). So at the proper time, grace and truth entered history in the person of Christ. The moment that Christ died on the cross, the veil in the temple was torn in two, signifying free access to God for all humanity. Since Christ was the perfect sacrifice, now by grace we receive salvation through faith. The law can no longer enslave and condemn us, because God's kindness and love through Christ justifies us. Believing this great message assures us of a new life here on earth and an eternal life with our Lord in heaven. This is God's gracious gospel. John Newton called grace "amazing," and truly it is.

Salvation at the Cross

1. We have seen that God longs to be gracious to us. Since the beginning, God has reached out to us. Read these gracious invitations and identify the free gift offered.

Isaiah 55:1–3, 6–7

John 3:16

Revelation 22:17

2. The substitutionary death of Christ on the cross established the new covenant. Study these Scriptures and describe how reconciliation and justification have been accomplished.

Romans 5:6–11

Ephesians 1:3–10

Hebrews 9:11–22

In order for anyone to stand securely and be at peace before a holy and just God, that person must be righteous. Hence, our need for justification. Remember the definition of justification? It is the sovereign act of God whereby He declares righteous the believing sinner while still in his sinning state. It doesn't mean that the believing sinner stops sinning. It doesn't even mean that the believing sinner is *made* righteous in the sense of suddenly becoming perpetually perfect. The sinner is *declared* righteous. . . . By grace, through faith alone, God declares the sinner righteous (justification). And from that moment on the justified sinner begins a process of growth toward maturity (sanctification).[2]

Charles R. Swindoll

Salvation Through Faith

3. The grace of God is absolute undeserved favor. In the following Scriptures, study the provision God has made to reconcile us to Him.

Romans 3:21–31

Romans 4:13–25

4. God's grace is fully revealed in the Cross. When we enter into His new covenant, how does God change our standing before Him?

We often speak of salvation in terms of "God's part and our part." However, this approach might suggest that we do, in fact, contribute to our salvation. . . . John R. W. Stott speaks to this: "We must never think of salvation as a kind of transaction between God and us in which He contributes grace and we contribute faith. For we were dead and had to be quickened before we could believe. No, Christ's apostles clearly teach elsewhere that saving faith too is God's gracious gift." Lutheran theologian Rod Rosenbladt says that, to the question "Don't we contribute anything to our salvation?" Scripture answers, "Yes, your sin!"[3]

Michael Horton

Faith, Not Works

5. Paul repeatedly declared the message that our salvation is by grace through faith, not by works. How do the following Scriptures convey this declaration?

Romans 4:1–5

Galatians 2:15–21

2 Timothy 1:8–10

Here is a spiritual principle regarding the grace of God: *to the extent you are clinging to any vestiges of self-righteousness or are putting any confidence in your own spiritual attainments, to that degree you are not living by the grace of God in your life.* This principle applies to salvation and in living the Christian life. . . . Grace and good works (that is, works done to earn favor with God) are mutually exclusive. We cannot stand, as it were, with one foot on grace and the other on our own merit.[4]

Jerry Bridges

6. We cannot cling to grace while relying on our own merits. Why do you think the Scriptures are so emphatic about the truth that God's saving work has nothing to do with our efforts? Use Ephesians 2:8–9 as a reference.

Author's Reflection

I was twelve years old when I experienced God's grace. I publicly stated my belief that Jesus Christ was the Son of God and that He died for the forgiveness of my sins. I didn't understand grace, but I did respond to God's great love and kindness to me. I understood the extraordinary cost of God's love for me. I wanted God to know that I believed in Him and that I loved Him for loving me so much.

Several years passed before I began to comprehend that Christ lived in me. I will never forget the day I realized that I didn't have to live life on my own. I was stressed and discouraged mainly because I was living life in my own strength—and I was running out of strength. I was trying so hard to be perfect and to hold everything together. Essentially, this is what living under the law is—striving to do in our own strength and power what God asks.

As I cried out to the Lord, He very gently spoke to my heart and asked if I would let Him be my Lord. Would I relinquish control, and give up thinking that I could live life apart from His life in me? That very day I recognized the truth of Paul's testimony in Galatians, "For when I tried to keep the law, I realized I could never earn God's approval. So I died to the law so that I might live for God. I have been crucified with Christ. I myself no longer live, but Christ lives in me. So I live my life in this earthly body by trusting in the Son of God, who loved me and gave himself for me" (Gal. 2:19–20 NLT).

For the first time, I knew that the living God, in His grace, had taken possession of His child. I was appropriating not only God's saving grace, but His indwelling Holy Spirit to enable me to live each day not in my own strength, but in His.

Trust is the lifeblood of faith; there is no saving faith without it. The Puritans were accustomed to explain faith by the word "recumbency." It meant leaning upon a thing. Lean with all your weight upon Christ. It would be a better illustration if I said: Fall at full length and lie on the rock of ages. Cast yourself upon Jesus. Rest in Him. Commit yourself to Him. That done, you have exercised saving faith.[5]

Charles H. Spurgeon

Amazing Grace

7. Charles Swindoll writes, "There is one and only one password for entering heaven: Grace."[6] Think about this amazing password. Has it become a part of your life? Whether you are asking God for the first time or thanking Him for what He has already done, write a prayer expressing your response to His gracious provision of eternal life.

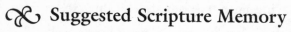 **Suggested Scripture Memory**
Ephesians 2:8–9

CHAPTER 5
Set Free by Grace

Sin is no longer your master, for you are no longer subject to the law, which enslaves you to sin. Instead, you are free by God's grace.
Romans 6:14 NLT

They travel lightly whom God's grace carries.[1]
Thomas à Kempis

$\mathcal{G}$od is the God of all grace. He always has been and always will be—His covenants guarantee it. In His grace, He sent His Son to redeem us. Christ's death purchased us, forgave us, freed us. The Cross accomplished our salvation and discharged us from the law. There is no need for continued sacrifices to atone for sin or to earn favor. The power of sin has been broken, and our sins are forgiven. Now we live in the newness of life by the power of the Holy Spirit, to the glory of God. The law said, "Live (do) righteously and you will be blessed." Grace says, "You are richly blessed; now (by faith) live righteously." It is imperative that we do not confuse law and grace. Traveling lightly depends upon it.

Free from the Power of Sin

1. Paul declared a powerful effect of believing in Christ's work of atonement. Read Romans 6 and summarize his teaching on our freedom from the power of sin. (For additional insights, read Galatians 2:19–21.)

Each moment of every day we choose whom we wish to follow. If it's the Savior, the benefits are many. If it is sin, the consequences are destructive and miserable. Then where does grace enter into this equation? Quite simply, grace makes the choice possible.

Before Christ, we had no choice. Sin was our one and only route. All of life was marked by unrighteousness. But once we came to the Cross and gave the Lord Jesus the right to rule our lives, we were granted a choice we never had before. Grace freed us from the requirement to serve sin, allowing us the opportunity to follow Christ's directives voluntarily. So as long as we do this, *we will not sin!* But as soon as you or I compromise with His mastery over us, the old master stands ready to lure us into sin.[2]

Charles R. Swindoll

2. Although the power of sin has been broken, we cannot say we have no sin. Read 1 John 1:5—2:2 and write down what the new covenant provides for us when we do sin.

Free from Bondage to the Law

3. It is critical for us to grasp the scope of God's grace, particularly in regard to the claims of the law. How do the following Scriptures help you understand your relationship to the law?
Romans 6:14

Romans 7:4–6

Romans 8:1–4

Galatians 5:18

4. Paul marveled that the Galatian church could so quickly desert the gospel of freedom in Christ for a distorted gospel presented by Jewish legalists (Gal. 1:6–7). Study Galatians 4:21—5:6 and record Paul's argument for our freedom in Christ.

5. Grace offers incredible benefits—freedom from condemnation and power to live righteously. How can understanding these concepts affect your day-to-day living?

> The proof that your old man is crucified with Christ is the amazing ease with which the life of God in you enables you to obey the voice of Jesus Christ.[3]
>
> *Oswald Chambers*

Author's Reflection

Jesus, full of grace and truth, was in the temple. The Jewish legalists, seeking to trap Him, brought to Him a woman caught in the act of adultery. The Law spoke to Grace: "She has broken the law. The law says she should die. What do you say?"

Grace replied to the Law, "If you have not sinned, you can stone her."

And because the law reveals sin, those who were under it were exposed, and they left.

Grace turned to the sinner and asked, "Where are your accusers? Is there no one who condemns you?" The sinner, in the presence of Grace, saw that she was no longer accused. Then she heard the pronouncement of freedom and forgiveness: "Neither do I. Go and sin no more."

There are some things in my life that can make me feel as if I've been accused, dragged into a court of law, and flung before the judge. Criticism is one of them. On one occasion after I finished speaking, I was on my way out to a car waiting to take me to the airport. Amid smiles and hugs all around, one dear woman rushed up to me and asked for my address.

"Oh, of course!" I said warmly.

As I was jotting it down for her she commented, "I need to give this to my friend because she wants to write to you. She didn't agree with what you said."

This remark echoed in my mind all the way back on the plane. I felt deeply discouraged, and I was plagued by questions. *Where did I go wrong? What did I say that was not the truth?* Someone had criticized me, and it made me feel like a failure. The earlier affirmations were far outweighed by this one response.

The criticism was particularly painful because it triggered a feeling that it was not acceptable for me to have any shortcomings—I had to be perfect. If I were to continue to speak publicly, I would be exposed to more criticism, more condemnation. It would be glaring evidence that perhaps I had no right to get up in front of people.

When we sin, the condemnation of the law makes us feel hopelessly cut off from relationship with God. It tells us that if we are not perfect, we can't stand before Him. "Do not sin and you will not be condemned," says the law. It is an impossible standard.

Under the new covenant, when we sin we hear this proclamation of grace: "You are no longer condemned. You are free. I love you, and I am for you. Confess your sin, and then go and live righteously without fear." Grace enables us to stay free. It is the only way to travel lightly.

[Both] forgiveness and repentance flow from the same source and are given by the same Savior. The Lord Jesus in His glory bestows both on the same persons. You can find neither the remission nor the repentance elsewhere. Jesus has both ready, and He is prepared to bestow them now and to bestow them most freely on all who will accept them at His hands. . . . Faith is as much the gift of God as is the Savior upon whom that faith relies. Repentance of sin is as truly the work of grace as the making of an atonement by which sin is blotted out. Salvation, from first to last, is of grace alone.[4]

Charles H. Spurgeon

Amazing Grace

6. "So if the Son sets you free, you will be indeed be free," declared Jesus (John 8:36 NLT). Compose a prayer to the Lord expressing your desire to live in the freedom that God's grace has made possible.

❧ Suggested Scripture Memory

Romans 6:14

CHAPTER 6

LIBERTY AND LEGALISM

❧

Jesus therefore was saying to those Jews who had believed Him, "If you abide in My word, then you are truly disciples of Mine; and you shall know the truth, and the truth shall make you free."

John 8:31–32 NASB

We may be seeking for our growth in a more diligent use of the means of grace, and a more earnest striving to live in accordance with God's will, and yet entirely fail. The reason is, that there is a secret root of evil which must be removed. That root is the spirit of bondage, the legal spirit of self-effort, which hinders that humble faith that knows that God will work all, and yields to Him to do it.[1]

Andrew Murray

*C*hrist teaches that as we abide in Him, we will know the truth—for He Himself is Truth. It is the *truth* that sets us free. As we begin to understand our freedom in Christ, it is important that we always base our freedom on biblical truth—not on traditions or on others' opinions of what is true. As we take in the teaching of others, we must always listen carefully and then filter their insights through the Scriptures. Does the Word forbid this? Does the Word grant this freedom? What does the Word say about this facet of the Christian life? It grieves the Lord when we burden ourselves with "untruth," which leads either to legalism or to unbiblical license. Christ came to set us free. He wants us to walk with Him in joy and freedom.

Christian Liberty

1. Part of Paul's encouragement to the church in Corinth was a reminder of their freedom in Christ. Read 2 Corinthians 3:12–18 and record Paul's teaching about the nature of Christian liberty and the means by which we experience it.

2. "Christian liberty," wrote Charles Ryrie, "is the new position in Christ of freedom from the bondage of sin and of the flesh."[2] With this definition in mind, read Galatians 5:13–26 and write down Paul's assessment of the struggle the Galatians were having and the remedy he proposed for their problem.

3. Our liberty in Christ affects our associations with others. Read Romans chapter 14 and 1 Corinthians chapter 8. Consider where in your life you can apply Paul's guidelines for relating to other believers.

[Just] as Paul moved, in Galatians 5, from telling the church to "stand firm" in its liberty and to "not let yourselves be burdened again by a yoke of slavery" (vv. 1–15), to informing them of how they have been freed in order to live for God and each other (vv. 16–26), so too we must use our liberty as an opportunity to glorify God and enjoy him forever. If we can enjoy an activity, a product, or a relationship that is within the guidelines of Scripture and do so as an expression of gratitude to the God who gave it, we are at liberty to accept these gifts from God's liberal hands.[3]

Michael Horton

The Encroachment of Legalism

4. Legalism is an attitude that enslaves us to believe that we must perform in order to win acceptance from God and others. Jesus perfectly exemplified liberty and a righteous response to the legalism of the law. Read Matthew 12:1–14 and indicate the ways He modeled liberty in the face of legalism.

5. Legalism seems to be uncomfortable with grace! In the following Scriptures, summarize the warnings concerning legalism's encroachment upon liberty and what is necessary to ensure our freedom.

Colossians 2:6–23

Hebrews 13:9

2 Peter 3:17–18

BECOMING A WOMAN OF GRACE

6. The bent to legalism is strong. Considering the passages you have looked at in this chapter, why do you think the Scriptures devote so much attention to this area of the Christian life?

But liberty does not mean license. It is a common charge of legalists that to teach grace without the restraint of the law means license to sin. This charge is untrue. To teach grace with restraint of the law is bondage. To teach grace is to teach a full and complete dependence upon God to provide according to His infinite love all that is needed by the one who places his trust in Him. The life of such a one must be a God-directed life. And a God-directed life is not one of carelessness and license. There is no indifference to sin in such a life. Only under grace can such a life be lived. But the one who imposes the law upon a believer, whether himself or another, by that very act denies the need of dependence upon God and thereby commits sin.[4]

J. F. Strombeck

7. From your experience, how would you describe the difference between legalism and liberty?

Author's Reflection

I like being told what is expected of me. I love it when some-one sets a standard and tells me exactly what I have to do to meet it. It gives me security, and I don't have to worry about whether my actions are "acceptable."

Keeping a set of rules ensures that I will always please peo-ple, and therefore I will never be ostracized. I want to fit in; I want to be accepted; I want to be thought of as part of the group. Living by a set of man-made codes also gives me a way to judge other people, so I can easily pick and choose with whom I fel-lowship.

Living a legalistic lifestyle, therefore, can feel comfortable and safe. I tend to lean toward this way of life because if I live by the rules, I can feel good about myself when others approve of my conformity. My desire to promote myself is communicated in small things such as worrying over whether my dress will meet with everyone's approval, or whether I have the right Bible, or if I quote from "acceptable" sources.

In these situations I find myself bound by other people's ideas of what is right rather than acting on my security in Christ and the freedom that His truth brings. For if I understand and accept my freedom in Christ, my purpose becomes to please God only. In all such issues of individual choice, my security lies not in how well I perform according to an external set of rules proposed by people. Rather, I can rest secure in the abiding presence of His Word and His indwelling Spirit to guide my choices. In exercising my liberty, the key criterion becomes, "If I do this, will it bring glory to God?"

The clearest picture of the difference between liberty and legalism can be found in Jesus' confrontations with the Pharisees. When He defended His disciples for gathering grain to eat on the Sabbath, or when He healed the withered hand of a man in the synagogue, He broke the man-made letter of the law and instead followed the Spirit of the law. He was not concerned about whether people were pleased with what He said or did. He was concerned only about the truth. Jesus acted out of freedom in the Spirit; the Pharisees acted out of bondage to the flesh. Jesus sought to please God from the heart; the Pharisees sought to earn favor from God and acceptance from men by their performance.

Legalism exalts the flesh and stifles the Spirit; liberty grounded in truth stifles the flesh and exalts the Lord.

The religious product being promoted by Judaizing interpolators was more self-control, more self-determination. If we engage in particular rituals and keep certain rules, we always know where we stand. If we know what we can do that will make us more acceptable in God's eyes than a person who doesn't do them, we, by doing them, can advance our status. Such a religion puts us in control. We no longer have to live by faith, trusting in God to accept us in mercy. We no longer have to live in love toward our neighbor, trusting, often against all appearances, that that neighbor is God's child. What we are being offered is a security system in which we do not have to live by faith, will not have to trust in God, but can trust instead in ourselves.[5]

Eugene Peterson

Amazing Grace

8. Charles Swindoll characterized Christian liberty this way: "My goal is not to please me, it is to please my Lord Jesus, my God. It is not to please you, it is to please my Lord."[6] Choose an area of your life in which you struggle with pleasing self or others instead of God. In a written prayer, ask God to lead you out of a legalistic spirit and into the freedom of His Spirit.

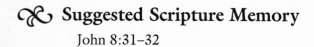 **Suggested Scripture Memory**
John 8:31–32

CHAPTER 7
The Law of Love

❧

This is My commandment, that you love one another, just as I have loved you.

John 15:12 NASB

Under the Mosaic system, love for others was to be in the degree in which one loved himself; under grace it is to be in the degree in which Christ has loved the believer and given His life for him. . . . Again, the standards of the teachings of grace surpass the standards of the laws of the kingdom.[1]

Lewis Sperry Chafer

*I*n God's provision of a new covenant we are no longer under the Mosaic law, but rather the law of Christ. What is this law? What are Christ's commands? How does His law differ from the old covenant? How are we to keep His law if it surpasses the Mosaic law? Now that we are under grace we must live as Christ has asked us, taught us, and empowered us to live. It can be summed up in one word: *love.* We are to love as we are loved by Christ. There is no more precious law than that of Christ. It is a gracious law that instructs and enables us to obey and live the highest and best life to the glory of God.

The Law of Christ

1. Jesus fulfilled the Mosaic law as He ushered in a new covenant. How do the following Scriptures define this new law?
John 13:34

John 15:12

Galatians 6:2

1 John 3:23

2. Scripture clearly states how the old law is fulfilled. What do the following verses teach about its relationship to the law of Christ?
Romans 13:8–10

Galatians 5:14–18

In relation to the Christian, the law, *as law*, having been completely fulfilled and satisfied in Christ, has been "done away." But as law it still remains to operate as an external restraint upon the ungodly. On the other hand, the law, *as inspired Scripture*, abides for all the saved and as such is "profitable" in all its parts. Only the soul saved by grace, understanding clearly what took place at Calvary, can truly delight in the law of the Lord. Such a one has seen in the cross the awful severity and doom of the law and rejoices in the assurance that its demands have been satisfied to the last farthing by the Lamb of God.[2]

Alva J. McClain

3. In 1 Corinthians 9:19–23, Paul makes a powerful statement concerning his relationship to others and to the law. Read this passage and write down how Paul sought to fulfill the law of Christ.

4. Paul's strong sense of grace in his own life freed him to relate to all people, regardless of their background, in order to share the gospel with them. How can his example influence the way in which you are involved with others?

Walking by the Spirit

5. To love others as Christ loves us is a high calling. What clues to fulfilling this command do you discover in the following Scriptures?

Romans 13:14

Galatians 5:25–26

Hebrews 4:14–16

Hebrews 12:14–15

We are responsible to clothe ourselves with Christlike character, but we are dependent on God's Spirit to produce within us His "fruit." We cannot make one inch of progress in sanctification apart from the powerful working of the Spirit in us. And He does this, not because we have earned it with our commitment and discipline, but because of His grace.[3]

Jerry Bridges

6. If we are to love others as Christ loved us, we must understand the work of grace in our lives. Read Matthew 18:21–35 and explain the ways in which grace was given and withheld.

7. The indebted slave "missed," or came short of, grace. Although he received grace, he did not extend it. How can we (either individually or collectively within Christian community) "see to it that no one misses the grace of God" (Heb. 12:15 NIV)?

Where the grace of God is missed, bitterness is born. But where the grace of God is embraced, forgiveness flourishes. . . . Hatred will sour your outlook and break your back. The load of bitterness is simply too heavy. Your knees will buckle under the strain, and your heart will break beneath the weight. The mountain before you is steep enough without the heaviness of hatred on your back. The wisest choice—the *only* choice—is for you to drop the anger. You will never be called upon to give anyone more grace than God has already given you.[4]

Max Lucado

8. The desire for justice can be a hindrance to loving others. What do these verses tell us about how we are to handle our desire for justice?

Romans 12:16–21

1 Peter 2:21–25

Paul's argument is that we should not take vengeance, because vengeance belongs to the Lord. And to motivate us to lay down our vengeful desires he gives us a promise—which we now know is a promise of future grace—"'I will repay,' says the Lord." The promise that frees us from an unforgiving, bitter, vengeful spirit is the promise that God will settle our accounts. He will do it more justly and more thoroughly than we ever could. Therefore we can back off and "leave room for God" to work.[5]

John Piper

Author's Reflection

In a "Peanuts" episode by cartoonist Charles Schulz, Lucy declared to Linus, "I love mankind; it's people I can't stand." I readily understand Lucy's dilemma. I can be so committed to loving others when I am alone, but let me go out of my room and I am continually challenged to be kind and loving.

As I have tried to understand why it is hard for me to love others sincerely, I have come to realize the depth of my selfishness and strong commitment to protect my "rights." I have a right to be loved first; I have a right to be treated kindly; I have a right not to suffer; I have a right to repay those who hurt me. Why should I love those who are unkind? How can I love those who wound me? How can I be expected to lay down *my* life for those who don't appreciate me? Why should I be asked to love others, not just as I love myself, but as Christ loves me, unconditionally—no *ifs*, *ands*, or *buts*?

It is hard, but it is the law of Christ. And if I am His child and I want to please Him, I need to obey. But *why* is this the law of Christ? Why are we asked to fulfill this one command? One of the reasons we are asked to love in this way is that it is the very best way for us to live. Love is the excellent way. Love heals. Love blesses not only the recipient but also the giver. It frees the lover from having to protect self. Love is full of grace.

Anger and bitterness destroy and divide. Anger and bitterness demand retribution and require great emotional energy. They produce anxiety, tension, and loss of hope. God doesn't want us to live this way. *It is because He loves us that He has commanded us to love.* We can love because we are loved perfectly by Him. His love is enough. He is our protector and shield; we no longer have to defend ourselves or battle for our rights. He has promised to repay any wrongs we have suffered. We are free to experience the freedom and blessing of forgiveness. We can rest in His justice and mercy. We can now just love and be loved—because He is the God of all grace.

> To the saint, personal insult becomes the occasion of revealing the incredible sweetness of the Lord Jesus. . . . Every time I insist upon my rights, I hurt the Son of God. . . . The disciple realizes that it is his Lord's honour that is at stake in his life, not his own honour.[6]
>
> *Oswald Chambers*

Amazing Grace

9. "Love is patient, love is kind," Paul declared (1 Cor. 13:4 NASB). Meditate on 1 Corinthians 13:4–7. Communicate to the Lord your need of His grace in loving others as He asks you to do.

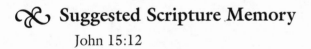 **Suggested Scripture Memory**
 John 15:12

$\mathscr{F}$REEDOM TO $\mathscr{S}$ERVE

*For you, dear friends, have been called to live
in freedom—not freedom to satisfy your
sinful nature, but freedom to serve one
another in love.*

Galatians 5:13 NLT

Man is permitted to *do* nothing until God has *done all*
that His grace designs. "Good works" grow out of, and
are made possible by, the gracious work of God.[1]

Lewis Sperry Chafer

$\mathcal{G}$race grants us freedom from sin and the flesh, and it grants us freedom to love and to serve. As we begin to serve, it is easy to focus on what we are doing and to measure our worth to God by our activity. Our service can often become a burden, robbing us of our freedom in Christ. How do we find the right balance? How do "good works" fit into our lives? We start by understanding that our faith does not consist in serving to earn favor with God or people. As a result, we will serve others in freedom, to the glory of God.

Doers of the Word

1. Essentially, *service* is obedience to God's direction in our lives. James speaks eloquently concerning *doing*. Summarize his teaching in James 1:22–27.

2. James continues his teaching on loving and serving others in James 2:1–13. How does he instruct us to live by the law of liberty?

James directs Christians to govern and conduct themselves more especially by the law of Christ. . . . This will teach us, not only to be just and impartial, but very compassionate and merciful to the poor; and it will set us perfectly free from all sordid and undue regards to the rich. . . . *We are under the law of Christ.* It is a *law of liberty,* and one that we have no reason to complain of as a yoke or burden; for the service of God, according to the gospel, is perfect freedom; it sets us at liberty from all slavish regards, either to the persons or the things of this world.[2]

Matthew Henry

3. James strongly emphasizes impartiality in our relations with others. Why do you think the Scriptures speak so explicitly to this aspect of serving one another in love?

The Works of Grace

4. Grace enables a new life in Christ. What do the following passages indicate this new life is to include?
Ephesians 2:4–10

Titus 3:4–8

5. In the Sermon on the Mount, Jesus taught about the importance of doing good. Read His words in Matthew 5:13–16 and describe the intended purpose for the service to which God calls us.

Works *follow* faith. Behavior *follows* belief. Fruit comes *after* the tree is well-rooted. Martin Luther's words come to mind: "No one can be good and do good unless God's grace first makes him good; and no one becomes good by works, but good works are done only by him who is good. Just so the fruits do not make the tree, but the tree bears the fruit. . . . Therefore all works, no matter how good they are and how pretty they look, are in vain if they do not flow from grace."[3]

Charles R. Swindoll

6. Since we are to do good works, we need to have an accurate understanding of how these "works" relate to faith. What insights do you find in James 2:14–26?

> James did not say that works are *essential* to faith, or that faith is unimportant. His argument was that works are *evidence* of faith. . . . He has simply said that genuine faith is accompanied by good works.[4]
>
> *J. Ronald Blue*

7. After studying these Scriptures, how would you describe the place of "works," or service, in your life in the context of grace and faith?

Author's Reflection

Trying to be perfect, wanting to please God, serving the body of Christ adequately—I often find that all these desires become blurred and I grow confused about how much or how little I must *do*. I don't always bridle my tongue; I rarely visit orphans and widows; I don't love impartially. I assume that I must try harder and do more to make up for my lack of obedience.

At this point Grace exclaims, "No! You now live in my realm of freedom, and you have the ever-present strength and help of the Holy Spirit. You must not try harder; you must strive less. You must acknowledge your helplessness and total dependence upon the Spirit for your guidance, your area of service, and your ability to love. You are created for good works, but they must flow out of your abiding communion with the living Vine."

Just as Mary of Bethany sat at the feet of Jesus listening to His words (while Martha was serving anxiously), Mary could not help but rise up and serve her Lord. It was her love for Jesus that moved her to abide in Him. As she abided, she was prompted to take her alabaster jar of perfume to anoint the Lord for burial—an incredible act of service that will always be told in remembrance of her.

True service always finds its source in loving our Savior, wanting to hear His Word, and then promptly obeying. As we listen to the Lord in faith with a willing heart, He can use us and produce

His fruit in us. Our major work is to trust, abide, and obey. This is freedom from the law, and it is freedom to serve. My trust and faith in walking in the Spirit, and my love for the Lord, will assure my good works.

Under a sense of legalism, obedience is done with a view to meriting salvation or God's blessing on our lives. Under grace, obedience is a loving response to salvation already provided in Christ, and the assurance that, having provided salvation, God will also through Christ provide all else that we need.

There is no question that obedience to God's commands prompted by fear or merit-seeking is not true obedience. The only obedience acceptable to God is constrained and impelled by love, because "love is the fulfillment of the law." God's law as revealed in His Word prescribes our duty, but love provides the correct motive for obedience. We obey God's law, not to be loved, but because we are loved in Christ.[5]

Jerry Bridges

Amazing Grace

8. "The idea is not that we do work for God, but that we are so loyal to Him that He can do His work through us," wrote Oswald

Chambers.[6] Do you struggle with "anxious service," or any other aspect of serving God and others? Express your thoughts to God concerning the amazing freedom He has given you to serve in response to grace, not out of a need for approval.

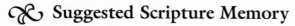 **Suggested Scripture Memory**
Galatians 5:13

CHAPTER 9

GROWING IN GRACE

*For the grace of God that brings salvation
has appeared to all men. It teaches us to say
"No" to ungodliness and worldly passions,
and to live self-controlled, upright and godly
lives in this present age, while we wait for the
blessed hope—the glorious appearing of our
great God and Savior, Jesus Christ, who
gave himself for us to redeem us from all
wickedness and to purify for himself a
people that are his very own, eager to
do what is good.*

Titus 2:11–14 NIV

"Sanctify" can stand for the accomplished work of God
applied to an individual in salvation . . . but sanctification also can refer to the working of the Word and the
Spirit to equip us to serve God in the world and to be
morally blameless until Jesus returns.[1]

Lawrence O. Richards

Grace not only brings the good news of the gospel, it instructs us in how to live. We can never say, "Well, I really didn't know how I was supposed to behave." By grace we are saved, and by grace we learn to live righteously. This world is not our ultimate home. We are pilgrims passing through to a greater kingdom. While we are here, we are to live in a way that glorifies God. A great incentive to godly living in our present age is our hope for the Lord's return. Paul describes it as a "blessed hope": it encourages us to live in such a way that we will not be caught off guard or embarrassed by the Lord's appearing. It motivates us to grow in grace.

Living Righteously

1. The new life enabled by grace is one that honors God. Read Titus 2:11–14 and describe the life of the believer who lives under grace.

2. As Christians, we live *in* the world, but we are not to be *of* it. How do these Scriptures encourage us to "deny ungodliness and worldly desires"?

Romans 12:1–2

Ephesians 4:17–24

1 John 2:15–17

1 John 3:1–3

Holiness is in the spirit and of the Divine spirit. It is not in forms and ordinances. . . . It is not in prohibitions and self-denial. . . . Christ lives in men through the Spirit. He is no longer a model but a living Presence. Christian faith does not copy Him; it lives Him. Christ is not imitated, but reproduced. Life is sanctified because He possesses it, lives it, transforms it. The Spirit of God does not work upon us; He lives in us. This is the contrast between the *works* of the flesh and the *fruit* of the Spirit. . . . Fruit does not come by toil but by appropriation, assimilation, and abiding. Holiness makes life fruitful because it abides in the Living Word and gives free scope to the Spirit of Life.[2]

Samuel Chadwick

3. Think of an example from your own life of what it means to live a "self-controlled, upright and godly [life] in this present age" (Titus 2:12 NIV). Describe a choice you would make to say "No" to ungodliness and worldly passions.

Looking for the Blessed Hope

4. Paul wrote to Titus of the "blessed hope" we now have (Titus 2:13). Peter also commended our hope as Christians. Based on the following passages from his epistles, how would you describe this hope and the nature of its influence on our lifestyle?

1 Peter 1:13–16

2 Peter 3:10–14

What a shout shall that be when men and angels shall unite to cry, "Hallelujah, hallelujah, for the Lord God Omnipotent reigneth!" What a satisfaction will it be in that day to have had a share in the fight, to have helped to break the arrows of the bow, and to have aided in winning the victory for our

Lord! Happy are they who trust themselves with this conquering Lord, and who fight side by side with Him, doing their little in His name and by His strength![3]

Charles H. Spurgeon

5. The Lord's return will be glorious! How does looking for Christ's appearing help you to live "blamelessly" in today's world?

Continuing to Grow

6. Paul urged Timothy to "be strong in the grace that is in Christ Jesus" (2 Tim. 2:1 NASB), and Peter wrote, "but grow in the grace and knowledge of our Lord and Savior Jesus Christ" (2 Peter 3:18 NASB). What do the following Scriptures teach about how you can grow in the Lord?

Matthew 4:4

John 15:5

Acts 20:32

1 Corinthians 2:9–12 (See also John 14:26.)

The Spirit is in us and we are led by Him. He works upon our wills; He creates desires after holiness; He reveals sin to us in all its foulness and ugliness and creates aspirations after purity and the life of God. Not only that, He gives us strength and power, enabling us to do what we now want to do. . . . How does that happen? How does His leading take place within us? And what does He lead us to? Well, He leads us in many ways, but He leads us particularly through the truth. It is He who is the author of the truth and He leads us to it and gives us an understanding of it. And as He does so, we are being sanctified.[4]

Martyn Lloyd-Jones

7. Reflect on the gracious provision God has made for our sanctification (refer to the Scriptures you studied in question 6). In what ways are you responsible to appropriate these gifts of grace?

Author's Reflection

As I look back over my life, it is interesting to see the slow (because of me!) sanctification process that has taken place. When I first began to grow in Christ, I was taught to abide in His Word with a heart to obey. I was encouraged to listen to His Word daily and to be still in order to hear His voice through His Spirit. So began my journey toward this blessed hope.

I can give testimony to the power of the Word and the Spirit. God's faithfulness to mold and shape His children into holiness and godliness is an extraordinary work of grace. I remember when I was struck with God's desire for my holiness. I was reading Oswald Chambers's exhortation, "It is quite true to say—'I cannot live a holy life,' but you can decide to let Jesus Christ make you holy."[5] And that is what I asked, that I might be made holy. It is a process, and I am far from the goal, but I do desire to present my body as a living and holy sacrifice. *Sanctification* is a lovely word, but in reality it is a day-by-day commitment to persevere in God's strength, not my own.

As I have gotten older, the Lord's appearing has become more precious. I find myself desiring more than ever to be all that God wants me to be. We are marvelously privileged to be found by grace and loved to the extent that the Spirit abides within us to guide us and teach us how to live. By grace, "We're being shown how to turn our backs on a godless, indulgent life, and how to take on a God-filled, God-honoring life. This new life is starting right now, and is whetting our appetites for the glorious day when our great God and Savior, Jesus Christ, appears" (Titus 2:11–13 *The Message*).

If the manner of life under grace is superhuman, so, also, the provided enablement is supernatural, and is as limitless as the infinite power of God. . . . Too much emphasis cannot be placed on the fact that, since God has proposed the impossible

rule of life and provided the sufficient Spirit, the
believer's responsibility is thereby changed from being
a *struggle* of the flesh to being a *reliance* on the Spirit.
Grace thus introduces a new problem for the believer's
life which is wholly foreign to every aspect of the law.
It is the problem of the adjustment of the heart to the
holy presence of the Spirit, and of maintaining the
unbroken attitude of dependence on Him.[6]

Lewis Sperry Chafer

Amazing Grace

8. Consider the amazing grace of God's salvation, His commitment to your sanctification, and His desire for your holiness. Then
respond in a written prayer to this thought from John Piper: "Sin
is what you do when your heart is not satisfied with God."[7]

℘ Suggested Scripture Memory

Titus 2:11–14

CHAPTER 10

THE SUFFICIENCY OF GRACE

And He has said to me, "My grace is sufficient for you, for power is perfected in weakness." Most gladly, therefore, I will rather boast about my weaknesses, that the power of Christ may dwell in me.

2 Corinthians 12:9 NASB

A primary qualification for serving God with any amount of success, and for doing God's work well and triumphantly, is a sense of our own weakness . . .

"When I am weak then am I strong,
Grace is my shield and Christ my song."[1]

Charles H. Spurgeon

*O*ur weakness in knowing what is best for our lives has been evident since day one of the human race. But God graciously understands our frailty, and He does not leave us helpless. Because we are weak, He provides a Savior to give us a new life. He gives us His Holy Spirit, who strengthens us to persevere in our trials. The more we acknowledge our helplessness, the more we realize our great need for *all* of God's grace. The remarkable truth is that God's grace is all-sufficient—enough, ample, abundant!—whatever our need, whatever our trial, whatever our circumstances.

Sufficient Grace for Each Believer

1. God's ways are not our ways. One of God's ways of ministering to Paul was to send him a "thorn in the flesh." Read 2 Corinthians 12:1–10 and answer the following questions.

a. What was Paul's experience with the Lord (vv. 1–6)?

(Most commentators agree that the "man in Christ" [v. 2] was Paul himself.)

b. Why was the thorn sent to Paul (vv. 7–8)?

c. What did Paul do, and how did God reply (vv. 8–9)?

d. What was Paul's response to God's way of answering his prayer (v. 10)?

e. Why do you think Paul could say that he was content in his circumstances?

2. Paul would echo his faith in God's grace in other letters. What do these passages affirm about the source of our strength and the confidence we can have in all situations?

2 Corinthians 3:4–6

Philippians 4:10–13

And I see Paul one night in his own hired house in Rome. The crowd is gone. He is slowing down a bit. One arm is around young Timothy, the other is over on dear old Dr. Luke. As you listen in, you hear Paul saying, "Do you know, dear friends, I would not have missed the thorn"—and his voice hoarsens a bit with emotion, and he is silent; a hush comes over them, and then he goes quietly on—"for the glory-presence of Jesus that came with it."[2]

S. D. Gordon

3. Paul is certainly not the only one to endure a "thorn." How have you experienced God's grace in the midst of a trial?

Sufficient Grace for the Body of Christ

4. God provides grace for each of us individually, and He also provides grace for us collectively in the community of believers. In our trials we need others to encourage and minister to us. As you read these Scriptures, write down Paul's key teachings concerning God's provision of spiritual gifts for each of His children. Romans 12:3–8

1 Corinthians 12:4—13:13

> Paul is most concerned to emphasise that whatever the gift, it must be used in love, which, indeed, entitles us to say that you should never estimate or judge a person's spirituality solely in terms of the gifts that are possessed.[3]
>
> *Martyn Lloyd-Jones*

5. Our commitment to serve the body is crucial to the church. What do the following passages indicate regarding the purposes for using our gifts?

Ephesians 4:7–16

1 Peter 4:10–11

6. The Scriptures affirm that each believer has been graciously gifted by the Holy Spirit. How does understanding the sufficiency of grace encourage you to serve the body of Christ?

Charisma is a special term for grace gifts. It focuses attention on how we are called to function within the body of Christ. God has given each believer a special endowment of the Spirit, so that he or she can make a distinctive contribution to individuals and to the community of faith. Living together, united by the bonds of brotherly love, each of us is used by God to enrich our brothers and sisters and to stimulate their growth to Christian maturity.[4]

Lawrence O. Richards

Author's Reflection

Jesus told us that in the world we would have tribulation, and certainly we do. I have learned to keep going in hard times because, just like Paul, I pray to God and He answers—most often with His grace and presence so that I can grow and He can be glorified. I think the key is trusting God enough to be content in the knowledge that He knows what is best for each situation. If it is not helpful for the "thorn" to be removed, then I must believe that enduring the thorn in the sufficiency of grace is for my highest good.

God is always enough. It doesn't matter what our circumstances are, and it doesn't matter if we think we are inadequate to serve the body. God has given us His grace, and it is sufficient. In a way, we are without excuse! We *can* persevere, and we *can* contribute to others.

It's interesting that God sent the thorn to Paul to keep him from pride. When Paul wrote about the gifts in Romans (12:35), he began by warning the believers to be careful about thinking of themselves more highly than they should. John Piper defines *pride* as "a turning away from God specifically to take satisfaction in *self*."[5] Pride has no place in grace or in the use of our gifts. Weakness and helplessness allow the Lord to work within us and to be honored.

The world equates weakness with failure. It is only grace that enables us to say that when we are weak, we are strong. Only grace makes us content with weakness. Only through grace can the power of Christ dwell in us. Only by grace do we receive special gifting to build up His body. And by grace alone our gifts are used in love to bless others.

If I can trust God for providing for my personal trials, I can certainly trust Him to equip me to be used according to His good purpose. I am probably more useful to others because of my trials, which have compelled me to appropriate His grace. I need to be a good steward of the gracious gifts I have received. They were given by the Spirit's sovereign design, and by His grace I can exercise them for the good of others. I do not need to feel inadequate, for my adequacy is from God. I do not need to feel incapable, because God, in His grace, has equipped me to serve the body. If I do feel weak, then that is good—for then the power of Christ can work through me, which will give Him glory.

Amazing Grace

7. John Piper stated, "His aim is that we grow deeper and stronger in our confidence that he himself will be all we need."[6] Write out a prayer asking God to help you understand the sufficiency of His grace.

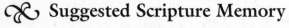 **Suggested Scripture Memory**

2 Corinthians 12:9

CHAPTER 11

$\mathcal{B}$ECOMING A $\mathcal{G}$RACIOUS $\mathcal{W}$OMAN

A gracious woman attains honor.

Proverbs 11:16 NASB

[If] this graciousness is the fruit of godly character, springing from a heart committed to the Lord, then such charm becomes a tool for drawing others to the Savior and for service to Christ in the kingdom. Such a "gracious" woman retains a great honor.[1]

$\mathcal{S}$ince we are the recipients of God's superabounding grace, since we are at liberty to love and serve, since we have divine enablement to live godly lives in this present age, then we need to be in the process of being known as women of grace. Because we have received grace, we should now exemplify graciousness. A gracious woman gains respect and honor, but any praise is lovingly given to the Lord. A gracious woman is concerned with the hidden person of the heart, a gentle and quiet spirit that is precious in the sight of the Lord. A gracious woman gives pleasure to God and to those she meets.

A Gracious Woman Gives Freely

1. A synonym for *gracious* is *benevolent* (the NIV translates it "kind-hearted" in Prov. 11:16). What do these verses say about gracious giving?

Proverbs 19:17

Proverbs 31:20

2 Corinthians 9:6–8

 God prizes not the size of the gift, but the giver's sincerity, spontaneity, and joyful willingness.[2]

David K. Lowery

A Gracious Woman Speaks Wisely

2. Kindness in speech should be a very noticeable characteristic of a woman of grace. How do these Scriptures encourage gracious conversation?

Proverbs 10:19

Proverbs 31:26

Ephesians 4:29–32

Colossians 4:5–6

3. In Colossians 4, Paul instructed that our communication should be "full of grace" and "seasoned with salt" (v. 6 NIV). Why do you think he chose the image of salt to portray gracious conversation?

In her tongue is the law of kindness; all she says is under the government of that law. The law of love and kindness is written in the heart, but it shows itself in the tongue; if we are kindly affectioned one to another, it will appear by affectionate expressions.[3]

Matthew Henry

A Gracious Woman Is Humble

4. "With the humble is wisdom," stated the writer of Proverbs (11:2 NASB). If we act and speak wisely and graciously, then humility will be evident in our lives. What do these passages teach about humility?

Philippians 2:1–11

1 Peter 5:5–7

Humility with regard to ourselves, then, consists in ascribing all that we are, all that we have, and all that we have accomplished to the God who gives us grace.[4]

Jerry Bridges

A Gracious Woman Rests in God

5. The Proverbs 31 woman clothes herself with the strength and nobility of Christ, and she smiles at the future (v. 25). There is a serenity and confidence about her. What assurances do these Scriptures provide of experiencing grace through resting in God? Isaiah 30:15

Romans 5:1–2

Philippians 1:6–7

1 Peter 5:10–11

Who could ever assure himself that he had accomplished *all* his Christian duty, or complied with *all* the demands found in the holy ideals of God? Who can repay God for the riches of His grace? To attempt to do so, is to place a sordid value on the priceless treasures of heaven's glory. God proposes to keep every believing soul, for He has said, "I will in no wise cast out." But His keeping will not be on the basis of exchange wherein Christian faithfulness, as important as it is, will be made the purchasing medium of the measureless goodness and blessing of God. He will keep by *grace* alone.[5]

Lewis Sperry Chafer

6. As you listen to God's invitation to live by grace alone, what area of your life do you see as needing God's grace the most? How can you begin to appropriate His grace?

Author's Reflection

At the heart of grace is *giving*. God is the giver of all good things. He delights to lavish blessings upon us. His grace is remarkable evidence of His generosity.

A gracious woman, therefore, is a *grace-giver*. She gives willingly—not just materially, but of herself:

- *Because she receives inexhaustible grace, she can extend grace.*
- *Because she is deeply loved by her Father, she can love others.*
- *Because she is forgiven, she can readily forgive.*
- *Because she hears the Lord speak graciously to her, she can communicate with grace.*
- *Because her strength and peace are from the Lord, she can impart a gentle and quiet spirit to those around her.*
- *Because she is humbled by the privilege of being God's child,*

she can serve selflessly, delighting in bringing glory to Him alone.

I tend to be a law-watcher, not a grace-giver. On a recent trip, my husband walked into our room and announced, with much frustration, that he had locked the keys in our rental car. Bless his heart, he heard his "lawful" wife respond to his discouragement with condemnation. "Honey, how could you have done that? You know you should never leave the keys in the ignition!" No grace extended, only censure for not being perfect.

To become a woman of grace means to be in the process of becoming more and more gracious. Grace should be so much a part of me that it spills over into every area of my life.

I have always been curious about why Paul began and ended each letter with some form of greeting or benediction of grace. In fact, the last verse of the Bible is, "The grace of the Lord Jesus be with all. Amen" (Rev. 22:21 NASB). Now, as I conclude this study, I think the reason why these epistles begin and end with "grace" is that *grace* is the beginning and the end. It ushers us into our life with God, and it will see us through to eternity. "'Tis grace hath brought me safe thus far," wrote John Newton, "and grace will lead me home." All of life can be summed up in the amazing truth that we are the beloved children of the God of all grace.

O Lord, You alone give abundant life. Deliver me from myself. Help me to see how destructive pride is, and how easily I revert to living under the law. Make me aware of how needful, dependent, and imperfect I am. May I continually be in awe of the abounding grace I receive from You. Enable me, Lord, to share Your grace with others. Thank You for never giving up on me. Thank You for Your grace that perfects, confirms, strengthens, and establishes me. May I become a woman of grace who is known for her giving spirit and for her love for You. May I become a gracious woman who attains honor for Your kingdom. I love You, Lord. Amen.

Grace walketh in simplicity, abstaineth from all show of evil, sheltereth not herself under deceits, doeth all things purely for God's sake, in whom also she finally resteth. . . . Grace faithfully attributeth all honour and glory unto God.[6]

Thomas à Kempis

Amazing Grace

7. "Grace is a way of life," asserted Lawrence O. Richards.[7] Paul beautifully stated his life's goal in Acts 20:24. Using this declaration as a guide, write out your desire to become a woman of grace.

❧ Suggested Scripture Memory
Proverbs 11:16

The grace of the Lord Jesus Christ,
and the love of God,
and the fellowship of the Holy Spirit,
be with you all.
2 Corinthians 13:14 NASB

The Father and the Child

The child spoke:

Father, I am overwhelmed by Your grace.

That is as it should be. May you always stand in awe of
My grace. What has meant the most to you?

*I think I see for the first time how truly helpless I am. It is
the height of presumption to try to rely on myself, my strength,
my performance, my flesh. Only in understanding how
totally dependent I must be, do I experience Your presence
and Your grace. The more I see my need for grace, the more
grace I receive.*

You have begun well, My child. How will you continue
to grow in My grace?

*As You instructed me in the beginning—by continuing to
listen carefully to Your Word, drawing close to You in
prayer, and walking daily in Your Holy Spirit.*

Good. My body needs women who exemplify My grace.
Remember that My grace is never-ending, and that I
delight in lavishing it on My children who walk with
Me.

I can think of no greater blessing, Father.

There is none—for I desire that you always know deep
within your heart that I am the God of all grace.

NOTES

Chapter 1—God Is Gracious

1. John Piper, *Future Grace* (Sisters, OR: Multnomah Books, 1995), 76.
2. Charles Caldwell Ryrie, *The Grace of God* (Chicago: Moody Press, 1963), 94.
3. Derek Kidner, *Psalms 73–150* (Downers Grove: InterVarsity Press, 1975), 307.
4. Lewis Sperry Chafer, *Grace* (Grand Rapids: Zondervan, n.d.), 4.
5. Piper, Future Grace, 80.
6. Matthew Henry, *Commentary on the Whole Bible* (Iowa Falls: Riverside, n.d.), vol. 4, 169.
7. Oswald Chambers, *My Utmost for His Highest* (Westwood, NJ: Barbour & Co., 1935), Dec. 19.
8. Andrew Murray, *The Two Covenants* (Fort Washington, PA: Christian Literature Crusade, 1983?), 3–4.
9. Chafer, *Grace,* 46.

Chapter 2—Covenants of a Gracious God

1. Murray, *The Two Covenants,* 5.
2. Lawrence O. Richards, *Expository Dictionary of Bible Words* (Grand Rapids: Zondervan, 1985), 194.
3. Ryrie, *The Grace of God,* 16–17.
4. Richards, *Expository Dictionary of Bible Words,* 199.
5. Murray, *The Two Covenants,* 13–14.
6. Alva J. McClain, *Law and Grace* (Winona Lake, IN: BMH Books, 1954), 30.
7. Murray, *The Two Covenants,* 13.

Chapter 3—The Law and the New Covenant

1. Robert Jamieson, A. R. Fausset, and David Brown, *Commentary on the Whole Bible,* rev. ed. (Grand Rapids: Zondervan, 1961), 1269.
2. Piper, *Future Grace,* 148–49.
3. Murray, *The Two Covenants,* 69–70.
4. Notes on Matt. 5:17, *The Woman's Study Bible: The New King James Version* (Nashville: Thomas Nelson, 1995), 1885.
5. Piper, *Future Grace,* 158.
6. Murray, *The Two Covenants,* 68–69.
7. Chafer, *Grace,* 4.

Chapter 4—God's Gracious Salvation

1. Jerry Bridges, *Transforming Grace* (Colorado Springs: NavPress, 1991), 23.
2. Charles R. Swindoll, *The Grace Awakening* (Dallas: Word, 1990), 44.
3. Michael Horton, *Putting Amazing Back into Grace* (Grand Rapids: Baker, 1991), 158–59.
4. Bridges, *Transforming Grace*, 33–34.
5. Charles H. Spurgeon, *All of Grace* (Springdale, PA: Whitaker House, 1981), 50.
6. Swindoll, *The Grace Awakening*, 36.

Chapter 5—Set Free by Grace

1. Thomas à Kempis, quoted in *The New Book of Christian Quotations*, comp. Tony Castle (New York: Crossroad, 1982), 102.
2. Swindoll, *The Grace Awakening*, 141.
3. Chambers, *My Utmost for His Highest*, Dec. 23.
4. Spurgeon, *All of Grace*, 105.

Chapter 6—Liberty and Legalism

1. Murray, *The Two Covenants*, 45.
2. Ryrie, *The Grace of God*, 79.
3. Horton, *Putting Amazing Back into Grace*, 202.
4. J. F. Strombeck, *Grace and Truth* (Moline, IL: Strombeck Agency, 1956), 76–77.
5. Eugene H. Peterson, *Traveling Light* (Colorado Springs: Helmers & Howard, 1988), 128.
6. Swindoll, *The Grace Awakening*, 171.

Chapter 7—The Law of Love

1. Lewis Sperry Chafer, *Systematic Theology* (Dallas: Dallas Seminary Press, 1948), vol. 4, 187.
2. McClain, *Law and Grace*, 72.
3. Bridges, *Transforming Grace*, 116.
4. Max Lucado, *In the Grip of Grace* (Dallas: Word, 1996), 155–57.
5. Piper, *Future Grace*, 264.
6. Chambers, *My Utmost for His Highest*, July 14.

Chapter 8—Freedom to Serve

1. Chafer, *Grace*, 10.
2. Henry, *Commentary on the Whole Bible*, vol. 4, 979–80.
3. Swindoll, *The Grace Awakening*, 47.
4. J. Ronald Blue, "James 2:14–26," *The Bible Knowledge Commentary:*

New Testament Edition, ed. John F. Walvoord and Roy B. Zuck (Wheaton, IL: Victor, 1983), 826.

5. Bridges, *Transforming Grace,* 92.

6. Chambers, *My Utmost for His Highest,* Dec. 18.

Chapter 9—Growing in Grace

1. Richards, *Expository Dictionary of Bible Words,* 543.

2. Samuel Chadwick, *The Way to Pentecost* (Avonmore, PA: The West Publishing Co., n.d.), 87.

3. Charles H. Spurgeon, *Morning and Evening* (McLean, VA: Macdonald Publishing Co., n.d.), Dec. 24, Evening.

4. Martyn Lloyd-Jones, *God the Holy Spirit: Great Doctrines of the Bible,* vol. 2 (Wheaton, IL: Crossway Books, 1997), 232.

5. Chambers, *My Utmost for His Highest,* July 9.

6. Chafer, *Systematic Theology,* vol. 4, 190–91.

7. Piper, *Future Grace,* 9.

Chapter 10—The Sufficiency of Grace

1. Spurgeon, *Morning and Evening,* Nov. 4, Morning.

2. S. D. Gordon, *Five Laws that Govern Prayer* (New York: Fleming H. Revell, 1925), 56–57.

3. Lloyd-Jones, *God the Holy Spirit,* 267.

4. Richards, *Expository Dictionary of Bible Words,* 307.

5. Piper, *Future Grace,* 87.

6. Ibid., 347.

Chapter 11—Becoming a Gracious Woman

1. "Graciousness: A Complement to Beauty," *The Woman's Study Bible: The New King James Version* (Nashville: Thomas Nelson, 1995), 1037.

2. David K. Lowery, "2 Corinthians 9:6–7," *The Bible Knowledge Commentary: New Testament Edition,* ed. John F. Walvoord and Roy B. Zuck (Wheaton, IL: Victor, 1983), 575.

3. Henry, *Commentary on the Whole Bible,* vol. 3, 976.

4. Jerry Bridges, *The Practice of Godliness* (Colorado Springs: NavPress, 1983), 97.

5. Chafer, *Grace,* 63.

6. Thomas à Kempis, quoted in *Giant Steps,* ed. Warren W. Wiersbe (Grand Rapids: Baker, 1981), 17–18.

7. Richards, *Expository Dictionary of Bible Words,* 320.

Also by Cynthia Heald

Becoming a Woman of Excellence (1986, NavPress)
Intimacy with God Through the Psalms (1987, NavPress)
Loving Your Husband (1989, NavPress)
Loving Your Wife, with Jack Heald (1989, NavPress)
Becoming a Woman of Freedom (1992, NavPress)
Becoming a Woman of Purpose (1994, NavPress)
Abiding in Christ: A Month of Devotionals (1995, NavPress)
Becoming a Woman of Prayer (1996, NavPress)
A Woman's Journey to the Heart of God (1997, Nelson)
A Journal for the Journey (1997, Nelson)

LOOK FOR THE COMPANION VIDEO TO BECOMING A WOMAN OF GRACE

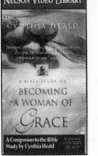

Becoming a Woman of Grace

As a companion to the Bible study, this video is the next best thing to having Cynthia Heald in the room. It brings her warm, friendly delivery and spiritual depth to your church or home. Focusing on God's grace, how to live in it, and how to extend it to others, this video will motivate you to truly become a woman of grace!

0-7852-7473-1 • VHS

ALSO BY CYNTHIA HEALD

A Woman's Journey to the Heart of God

With her characteristic personal warmth and solid biblical teaching, Cynthia Heald helps equip women for their spiritual journey as she shares her personal insights into the struggles and joys of a life devoted to walking with God.

0-7852-7239-9 • 256 pages • Hardcover

A Journal for the Journey

This journal is an interactive companion to A Woman's Journey to the Heart of God, designed to guide women as they personalize their spiritual journey.

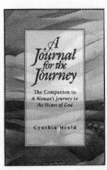

0-7852-7126-0 • 144 pages • Trade Paperback with Lay-Flat Binding